Thousand Oaks, California

The Medieval World

Manners and Customs
in the Middle Ages

Marsha Groves

Crabtree Publishing Company
www.crabtreebooks.com

Crabtree Publishing Company
www.crabtreebooks.com

Coordinating editor: Ellen Rodger

Series editor: Carrie Gleason

Project editor: L. Michelle Nielsen

Designer and production coordinator: Rosie Gowsell

Production assistant: Samara Parent

Scanning technician: Arlene Arch-Wilson

Art director: Rob MacGregor

Project development, editing, photo editing, and layout:
First Folio Resource Group, Inc.: Tom Dart, Greg Duhaney,
Sarah Gleadow, Debbie Smith

Photo research: Maria DeCambra

Consultant: Isabelle Cochelin, University of Toronto

Photographs: Alinari/Art Resource, NY: p. 12; Archivo
Iconografico, S.A./Corbis: p. 24 (left); Art Archive/Archivio di
Stato di Siena/ Dagli Orti: p. 22; Art Archive/Bodleian Library
Oxford/ Canon or 79 folio 2v: p. 23 (bottom); Art Archive/British
Library: title page, p. 5, p. 16 (left), p. 26 (bottom); Art Archive/
Médiathèque François Mitterand Poitiers/Dagli Orti: p. 26 (top);
Art Archive/Musée Condé Chantilly/Dagli Orti: p. 8 (bottom),
p. 9; Art Archive/San Alberto di Butrio Abbey Ponte Nizza/Dagli
Orti: p. 11 (top); Art Archive/University Library Heidelberg/
Dagli Orti: p. 15; The Barber Institute of Fine Arts, University of
Birmingham/ Bridgeman Art Library: p. 27;

Bibliothèque Nationale, Paris/Bridgeman Art Library: p. 13;
British Library/Add. 16979 f.21v: p. 17 (right); British Library/
Bridgeman Art Library: p. 11 (bottom), p. 25; British Library/
Cotton Cleopatra C. XI f.27v: p. 16 (right); British Library/Cotton
Vitellius A. XIII f.5: p. 14 (bottom); British Library/HIP/The
Image Works: p. 10, p. 17 (left); British Library/Sloan 2435 f.35:
p. 6; British Museum/Topham-HIP/The Image Works: p. 20
(bottom, all); Giraudon/Art Resource, NY: cover, p. 7 (bottom),
p. 24 (right); Granger Collection, New York: p. 14 (top), p. 18 (top),
p. 19 (bottom), p. 23 (top), p. 29; Erich Lessing/Art Resource:
p. 19 (top), p. 28; National Trust/Art Resource, NY: p. 18
(bottom); Réunion des Musées Nationaux/Art Resource, NY:
p. 20 (top); Scala/Art Resource, NY: p. 21; Snark/Art Resource,
NY: p. 7 (top); Victoria & Albert Museum, London/Art Resource,
NY: p. 8 (top)

Map: Samara Parent, Margaret Amy Salter

Illustrations: Jeff Crosby: pp. 30–31; Katherine Kantor: flags, title
page (border), copyright page (bottom); Margaret Amy Salter:
borders, gold boxes, title page (illuminated letter), copyright page
(top), contents page (background), pp. 4-5 (timeline), p. 4
pyramid, p. 32 (all)

Cover: In medieval times, the new bride and groom took part in
several processions with friends and family.

Title page: In a beautiful garden, a chivalrous man tells stories
and recites poems to the woman he loves.

Crabtree Publishing Company
www.crabtreebooks.com   1-800-387-7650

j 390.094

Cataloging-in-Publication Data
Groves, Marsha.
   Manners and customs in the Middle Ages / written by
 Marsha Groves.
      p. cm. -- (The medieval world)
Includes index.
ISBN-13: 978-0-7787-1357-9 (rlb)
ISBN-10: 0-7787-1357-1 (rlb)
ISBN-13: 978-0-7787-1389-0 (pb)
ISBN-10: 0-7787-1389-X (pb)
    1. Europe--Social life and customs--Juvenile literature.
    2. Civilization, Medieval--Juvenile literature. 3. Europe--
    History--476-1492--Juvenile literature. I. Title. II. Series.
GT120.G76 2005
390'.094--dc22   2005019027
                                                          LC

**Published in
the United States**
PMB 16A
350 Fifth Ave.
Suite 3308
New York, NY
10118

**Published
in Canada**
616 Welland Ave.
St. Catharines
Ontario, Canada
L2M 5V6

**Published in the
United Kingdom**
73 Lime Walk
Headington
Oxford
OX3 7AD
United Kingdom

**Published
in Australia**
386 Mt. Alexander Rd.
Ascot Vale (Melbourne)
VIC 3032

Table of Contents

4 The Middle Ages

6 Orders of Society

8 Noble Youth

10 At the Table

12 Chivalrous Knights

16 In a Monastery

18 A Woman's World

20 Wedding Customs

24 Birth and Death

26 Winter Festivities

28 Spring Holidays

30 Harvest Time

32 Glossary and Index

The Middle Ages

The Middle Ages, or medieval period, lasted from about 500 A.D. to 1500 in western Europe. During that time, kings, queens, and important nobles ruled. These great lords and ladies tried to increase their land and power by conquering, or taking over, other territories and by arranging marriages that united the ruling families of different regions.

Great lords and ladies were helped by less important nobles, called vassals. Vassals were given land in return for their promise to advise and fight for their lords and ladies.

Most medieval people were peasants. They lived in the countryside, where they farmed the vassals' land. Other people, such as craftspeople and merchants, lived in towns or cities. Craftspeople made items such as pottery, leather, and glass, while merchants traded cloth, spices, and other goods.

▶ *Medieval society was organized into different social levels, or ranks, with each level more powerful than those below. Most people did not move from one rank to another.*

March 25, an important Christian holiday called the Feast of the Annunciation, becomes New Year's Day, until the 1700s

567

The concept of chivalry, or the ideal behavior of a knight, is developed

1000s

The French author Chrétien de Troyes writes stories of chivalry about King Arthur and the Knights of the Round Table

1170s

Laws are passed to control the way people dress

1300s

700s
The Rule of St. Benedict, written around 530 A.D., becomes the most common guide for behavior in monasteries

1100s
Weddings become religious ceremonies

1250
Instruction books for good behavior gain popularity

During medieval times, many ideas about proper manners, as well as customs for celebrating holidays, came from religion. Christianity was popular throughout most of Europe, while Islam influenced the Middle East and northern Africa.

Showing Status

Medieval people showed their status, or position in society, by their manners. Stories, **sermons**, and instruction books described how people should act, speak, and dress, depending on their status.

Nobles and **priests** often criticized successful merchants and craftspeople for dressing and behaving as if they were as important as nobles. In the late Middle Ages, laws, called sumptuary laws, were passed in many cities to ensure that all people, especially merchants and tradespeople, dressed in ways appropriate to their status. People who broke sumptuary laws were fined.

Turkeys, brought to Europe from the Americas, quickly become a holiday food

1520

1400s
Table napkins start to become popular

▶ *Nobles were taught to speak in formal and courteous ways to those above them in rank. Formal speech was not expected from people of lower rank. They demonstrated their status by being respectful and obedient.*

Orders of Society

In medieval times, society was thought to be made up of three orders, or groups. There were those who fought, those who prayed, and those who labored.

Those who fought included kings, nobles, and knights. They used their military skills to try to ensure peace and justice. Those who prayed, such as priests, monks, and nuns, devoted their lives to prayer, religious study, and caring for the poor and sick. Peasants, tradespeople, craftspeople, and merchants were among those who labored, or worked.

Making Oaths

Medieval people made promises, also called oaths or vows, to show their commitments to other people and to causes. These commitments included supporting a king or noble, marrying, and becoming a monk or nun. By the early Middle Ages, many customs surrounded the making of oaths.

The most solemn oath was giving homage. Vassals, who were both men and women, promised to be faithful to their lords, to give them good advice when called upon, to provide men to fight in times of war, and to defend their lords' honor. In return, they received a portion of their lords' land to use and pass on to their **heirs**. Vassals also relied on their lord to defend their honor and property from those who wished to harm them.

▲ The monk in his habit, the knight in his armor, and the peasant in his rough woolen clothing each had different responsibilities and obligations to other people in society.

Giving Homage

During the act of homage, vassals usually knelt before their lords and placed their hands between their lords' hands. They swore oaths such as the following, "I will be your man from this day forward, and be faithful and true to you, and acknowledge that I hold this land from you, excepting only the duty I owe to the lord my king."

▼ *Even kings were sometimes vassals of other kings if they held territories within those kings' lands.*

Free Peasants and Serfs

Some peasants, called free peasants, swore oaths of fealty to their lords. With their right hands raised, they promised to pay rent and perform all required duties, such as helping bring in the harvest. Other peasants, called serfs, were bound to their lords by law, not by oath. Serfs were not free to leave their lord's land, and they owed him many obligations, including farming his fields. Serfs who wished to avoid this work had to pay fines, or small fees.

▲ *In return for swearing oaths, peasants were allowed to use the lord's land and were protected by him from harm.*

Noble Youth

Many noble families sent children over the age of seven to be raised and taught in other noble households. This custom was called fostering.

Fostering strengthened the bonds of friendship and loyalty between two families. By selecting foster families with power or skill in war, parents hoped to improve their children's chances for success in life.

In a Noble Household

Noble boys and girls learned what behavior was expected of them by sharing in the duties of running a noble household. They were trained to speak respectfully to those of higher status, using proper titles and bowing or kneeling. They also learned to supervise and command those below them in rank, such as servants and soldiers.

▲ Noble boys served the lord at mealtime. When they approached the table, they made an obeisance, or a small bow.

Pages and Squires

Noble boys began by working as pages, running errands and carrying messages. As they grew older, they served the lord, the lady, and their guests at feasts and other formal meals. In their teens, noble boys became squires, and were in training to be a knight. While assisting the lord and his sons, they learned to take care of weapons and armor, and to ride and care for horses.

◀ When noble boys first learned to fight, they practiced using blunt weapons made from wood. When they improved, they used real swords.

Serving the Lady

Noble girls served the lady of the household. They brought food to her private chamber, helped her bathe and dress, read to her, and prayed with her. The lady taught the girls to supervise the cook and other servants, to manage household expenses, to heal the sick and injured, to pray, and sometimes to read and write.

Training Non-Nobles

Like noble children, children of peasants and tradespeople began to prepare for their future jobs at a young age. Children as young as seven were sent to the homes of masters, or expert tradespeople. There they learned trades, such as weaving, metalworking, or carpentry. Children of parents who could not provide these opportunities, began a lifetime of work as household servants with simple jobs, such as turning the **spit** at the cooking fire.

▲ *Young ladies learned to* spin, sew, *and* embroider.

Books of Manners

Noble parents and teachers in wealthy households wrote instructions for proper behavior in guidebooks called books of manners. Here are one noble father's suggestions to his son, who was preparing to serve in the household of a high-ranking noble:

- When you enter a room, walk calmly and meet everyone's eyes.
- At mealtime, offer your lord water and towels so he can clean his hands.
- If people more important than you come to the table, back away and make space for them.
- Stand up straight — no lounging, leaning, or jiggling about.
- Do not sit down unless told to.
- Be humble and merry if you are asked to join the conversation.
- Be prepared to light the lord's way with a torch when he is ready to leave the table.

At the Table

Fine manners were important in medieval society and were considered a sign of noble status. Books of manners instructed people of high status, such as nobles and wealthy merchants, on proper behavior at mealtimes.

Politeness at the Table

People were expected to speak pleasantly at the table, and never to interrupt anyone or argue. Arguing was believed to be bad for digestion. Well-behaved people were "dainty" while eating, meaning neat and never greedy. Food was served on large platters that everyone shared. Out of courtesy, people offered other diners at the table the best bits of food from the platters.

At each person's place lay a slice of bread, called a trencher. The most important people had a slice of bread cut for them from a loaf set before their place, while others broke pieces off from a shared loaf. The bread was often used as a plate and as a scoop for eating stews and other foods. Good manners required breaking off just as much bread from your trencher as you could use and eat, so that leftover bread could be collected and given to the poor.

▲ Rich or poor, everyone used a small eating knife to serve themselves from common platters at mealtimes. Table forks were almost unknown in medieval Europe.

Cleanliness at the Table

Hands and fingernails were supposed to be clean at the table, as eating with one's hands was proper behavior at the time. Dirty hands and dripping noses were never to be wiped on the tablecloth or on napkins.

It was considered rude for people to clean their teeth while still at the table. Those who had rotten teeth, a common condition in the Middle Ages, were to avoid eating from shared platters.

▶ *Towels and water drawn from a well were brought to the table so that diners could clean their hands between courses.*

At a Muslim Table

In the Middle East, meals were a way to show hospitality to visitors and generosity to the poor. A **Persian** saying from the 900s A.D. explains: "Give all the food you have to your guest, even if you have only a drop of water for yourself."

Each meal began and ended by giving thanks to Allah, or God. The diners washed their hands, then the meal was served in several courses. It was considered rude to take large bites, to grab food from common platters, or to eat more than you needed. Hosts were taught to finish eating last so that guests did not feel rushed during the meal.

▶ *Muslims, or followers of Islam, used only the middle three fingers of their right hands to eat.*

Chivalrous Knights

Knights were medieval warriors who rode warhorses and fought with swords and lances. They led armies of foot soldiers, archers, and pikemen.

In the early Middle Ages, vassals who were skilled fighters could become knights by successfully supporting their lord in battle. By about 1000, only the sons of knights could become knights themselves.

The Rise of Chivalry

Warriors were not always easy to manage in times of peace. Greedy nobles who wanted more land sometimes used their armies to take over neighboring territories. Knights who had no land of their own sometimes seized people for **ransom**, robbed travelers, and stole food and valuables.

From about 1000 to 1200, new ideas about warriors' behavior were promoted by the Church and made popular in songs and stories. Instead of behaving brutally, a knight was expected to be well-mannered and self-disciplined. He was also expected to fight for Christian beliefs and for justice. This ideal behavior was called chivalry, from the French word *chevalier*, meaning "knight."

▲ *When armor began to cover more of a knight's face and body, knights added decorations, called coats of arms, to the armor to help others identify them.*

The Code of Chivalry

The code of chivalry encouraged knights to protect the weak, never to attack those who could not defend themselves, and to treat prisoners respectfully. Knights also had to live by a **moral** code that included keeping oaths, being truthful and generous, remaining loyal to their kings, lords, and ladies, and defending the Christian faith.

Becoming a Knight

A boy trained as a page, then as a squire in a noble household. When a noble thought his squire was ready to become a knight, usually between the ages of 15 and 21, a ceremony took place. In the early Middle Ages, a squire knelt before the noble, or overlord, who had raised him. The squire was dubbed, or given a strong blow to his shoulders, chest, or head, by the noble's open hand or the flat part of the noble's sword. Then, the squire was named a knight.

Over time, the dubbing ceremony became more formal and religious. Squires prepared for the ceremony with a **ritual** cleansing bath and a night of prayer. If the new knight was from a royal family, he was often dubbed in a church before a large audience.

▼ *After a knight was dubbed, he was given his own sword and spurs. Spurs are short spikes that a knight attached to the heels of his boots to make his horse go faster.*

13

The Samurai

In medieval times, warriors in many lands developed codes of honor. Samurai were warriors who served the powerful lords of Japan. In return for the samurai's loyalty, the lords paid them an income, which was usually money. Over time, rules of samurai behavior, called *bushido,* or the way of the warrior, developed. The **virtues** of the samurai, who were also called *bushi,* included bravery, loyalty, generosity, compassion for the weak, and a desire for justice. Samurai also valued truthfulness and keeping their promises.

Chivalry on the Battlefield

Knights were expected to behave in a chivalrous manner on and off the battlefield. In a medieval battle, noble fighters who were disarmed or injured often surrendered to their opponents. They trusted that the victorious knights would not kill them because the code of chivalry forbade attacking an unarmed person. Knights who surrendered gave their word of honor that they would not attempt to rejoin their armies, and those who were truly honorable did not break their promises.

▶ *Defeated knights remained with their captors until their families or supporters paid a ransom. Ransoms for kings and powerful nobles could be so large that the whole kingdom had to contribute to raise enough money.*

Tournaments

Tournaments were competitions in which knights displayed their skills before an audience. Jousts were one type of combat in tournaments. Knights armed with jousting lances, or long, wooden poles with blunt ends, galloped rapidly toward each other on horses. The goal was to knock an opponent off his horse or to injure him.

Melees were also popular. Melees were mock battles between two teams of knights. Points were earned when knights defeated opponents by doing things such as injuring them so much that they could not continue fighting.

A Knight and his Lady

Many rules of chivalry described a knight's duty to "his lady," a woman whom he admired and to whom he promised loyalty. Ladies were the wife of a knight's lord, or another woman from the **court**. Many knights fought in tournaments to impress their ladies. To show their interest, ladies gave their knights tokens of their affection, called favors. Favors were often embroidered cloths or ribbons that the knights attached to their armor.

▲ Noble ladies presented garlands, banners, or other prizes to knights who won tournaments.

Gologras and Sir Gawain

Chivalry was made popular in songs and stories, especially in the tales of King Arthur, Queen Guinevere, and the Knights of the Round Table. In *The Knightly Tale of Gologras and Sir Gawain*, King Arthur sends Sir Gawain, a young knight of the Round Table, to fight Gologras, an enemy who rules a neighboring kingdom. Gawain defeats Gologras, but returns to Arthur's court pretending to have lost, in order to save his opponent's reputation. Gologras is so moved by Gawain's kindness, and so impressed by Gawain's skill in battle, that he decides to become a member of King Arthur's court so that he too can learn true chivalry.

In a Monastery

Almost all medieval Europeans were Christians. Christians believe in one God and follow the teachings of Jesus Christ, who they believe is God's son.

In the Middle Ages, many people devoted their lives to religion. Some religious men, called monks, and women, called nuns, lived separately in communities called monasteries. Days in the monastery were organized around a schedule of religious services called the Divine Office. Monks and nuns studied the words and music of the Divine Office, and prayed and sang at many services each day. They also did the cooking, cleaning, and other work necessary to run the monastery.

▲ *The crown of a new monk's head was shaved in a style called a tonsure. This haircut was a symbol of the monk's commitment to a religious life.*

Following the Rule

Monks and nuns were expected to follow strict rules of behavior so that the monastery ran smoothly. The most popular set of rules was the Rule of St. Benedict. The Rule sets out a daily schedule for work and prayer, and teaches monks how to lead humble and unselfish lives. It is still in use today.

◀ *Monks and nuns spent many hours each day copying books by hand, as was usual in the Middle Ages. Many of these books were texts of church services and prayers.*

The Rule of St. Benedict

Here are some of St. Benedict's rules:

- Be silent whenever possible, speak softly when you need to, and never gossip.
- Look downward when walking, sitting, or standing, so that you think about your own actions and mistakes, rather than looking around for things to criticize.
- Never overeat or waste food, since taking more than you need could deprive someone else of food.
- Everyone must take turns working in the kitchen and serving fellow monks without complaining.
- Those who are sick should not be demanding. Those who care for them should be kind and patient.
- Never argue or insult anyone. Try always to be obedient and humble.

▲ *The Rule of St. Benedict was written around 530 A.D. by Benedict of Nursia, the abbot, or leader, of the monastery at Monte Cassino, in Italy.*

▲ *Monks and nuns rose early in the morning and went to the chapel to sing or chant the first service of the day, called Matins. The last service of each day, Compline, took place just before bedtime.*

Punishing Disobedience

Many monks and nuns did not choose religious life for themselves, but were placed in monasteries by their families. Some were very unhappy, and were often disobedient. Those who refused to obey the rules were punished by being isolated within the monastery. In isolation, they were forced to eat, work, and pray alone. If they complained, they were punished even more severely by being beaten with a thin rod in front of the whole monastic community.

A Woman's World

Women in the Middle Ages who did not devote their lives to religion were expected to marry and have children. They were also supposed to manage a household.

Women cooked and preserved food, made clothes for members of the household, and prepared or bought medicines for sick family members. When their husbands were fighting in wars or away on business, wives did many of their husband's jobs. Some women owned workshops or small businesses, or farmed alongside men in the fields.

Instructions for Wives

Some husbands, especially townspeople and less important nobles who were trying to gain status, wrote books instructing their wives on proper behavior. Wives were told to obey and care for their husbands. When the men arrived home, their wives were expected to greet them gently and sit them down by the fire. The women were to remove their husbands' shoes, offer them food and drink, and speak of pleasant matters.

▲ *Women from wealthy households chose, supervised, and disciplined the many servants who lived and worked in their homes.*

▶ *A husband and wife were expected to guide the religious behavior of all members of their household. Here, a husband prays with his wife by his side.*

Modesty

Modesty and self-discipline were considered a woman's most important qualities. She demonstrated these by her soft voice and calm expression, and by the quiet way in which she moved. A modest woman was expected to keep her opinions to herself, and never to interrupt or contradict anyone.

How to Dress

A woman was expected to dress according to her status, not to be messy, and never to spend more money on clothes and jewelry than her family could afford. Sumptuary laws told wives of rich merchants and peasants exactly how much gold jewelry they could wear, the types of fabrics they could use to make their clothing, and even how long the toes of their shoes could be.

▲ *In a woman, a gentle bend to the neck and graceful hand gestures were regarded as beautiful, and as signs of good manners.*

Muslim Women

During the Middle Ages, most people in southern Spain, North Africa, and the Middle East were Muslims. Like Christian women in Europe, Muslim women were expected to dress modestly. Most women wore loose-fitting clothing with high necklines, such as long robes or knee-length **tunics** over trousers. Muslim women also covered their hair, especially in public, and often used veils to cover their faces.

Wedding Customs

In the Middle Ages, a person's status influenced the age at which he or she married. Noble women often married early, as young as 14. Their husbands were usually much older.

Peasants, tradespeople, and merchants tended to marry in their twenties, once both partners were able to set up a home and support a family. Men usually waited until they had acquired a piece of land to farm, had been trained in a craft, or had established a business.

The Betrothal

In the Middle Ages, two people were betrothed, or promised to one another, before they were married. The period between the betrothal and the wedding was as short as a few weeks or as long as several years. In noble families, marriages were sometimes arranged by parents while children were still very young, so long betrothals were common.

▲ *At the time of the betrothal, a groom who could afford to, gave his future bride a ring as a sign of their promise to marry. In the late Middle Ages, the ring became part of the wedding ceremony instead.*

Rings and brooches engraved with romantic phrases, such as "With all my heart" or "I love you completely," were given as betrothal gifts.

The Betrothal Contract

A betrothal contract was made between the families of the groom and the bride. It listed the land, money, or other possessions, such as furniture or tableware, that the bride would bring to the marriage. This was called her dowry. The betrothal contract also explained how the groom's family would support the bride if her husband died, usually by giving her money or land.

▲ Accompanied by bagpipes, a procession joins the bride and groom on their way to the church.

Dressed for the Wedding

On the wedding day, the bride, groom, and guests wore their best clothes and jewelry. Nobles and the very wealthy wore garments embroidered with gold and jewels. Bright, rich colors were especially popular, and many brides were married in red or yellow.

The bride wore a wreath of flowers in her hair or, if she were wealthy, a wreath of jewels. Her hair was left loose and uncovered in public for the last time, since married woman covered their hair as a sign of modesty.

The Wedding Ceremony

In the early Middle Ages, most wedding ceremonies were simple and brief. In many parts of Europe, the bride's father held her right hand in his grasp until the couple had vowed to live faithfully together as husband and wife. Then, the father placed his daughter's hand on her new husband's. Usually, there was no official or priest present.

Beginning in the 1100s, the Church became more involved in marriage ceremonies. By the 1200s, a newly married couple was expected to go to church and be blessed by the priest immediately after saying their wedding vows. The priest met them at the porch of the church, made sure that the bride and groom had both freely agreed to the marriage, and blessed them. Sometimes, a special service called a nuptial, or wedding, mass then took place inside the church to celebrate the marriage.

▲ *At the wedding ceremony, the bride and groom stood before a few witnesses, usually family members or close friends, and promised to live together faithfully.*

The Wedding Procession

Once a couple had married, family and friends accompanied them as they walked to the wedding feast. This procession allowed the entire community to see that the couple had wed. Neighbors called out good wishes and threw grain or flowers over the bride and groom, to wish them a happy marriage with many children.

The Wedding Feast

All marriages, whether of peasants or nobles, were celebrated with a feast. At a simple peasant feast, guests ate roasted meat and sweet and **savory** baked pastries, and drank ale. Musicians from the village played, and everyone danced.

A royal wedding feast included many dishes designed to astonish the guests, such as pies with live birds tucked inside that flew out when the crust was cut, roasted swans decorated to look as if they were alive and swimming on a pond, and cakes baked in the shape of boats or castles.

▲ *A royal wedding feast was meant to impress and amaze the guests. Jugglers, acrobats, dancers, and musicians were hired to entertain those who attended.*

A Medieval Jewish Wedding

Some people in medieval Europe were Jewish, or followers of the religion of **Judaism**. On the morning of a Jewish wedding, the bride and groom were brought separately to the synagogue, the Jewish place of worship. They were accompanied by friends, family, and leaders of the synagogue.

At the door, the groom took the bride's hand, and they were showered with grain and coins for good luck. Inside the synagogue, the couple stood with their parents and their marriage was blessed. Family, friends, singers, and musicians joined the couple in a public procession to their new home, where a lively feast, with music and dancing, was held.

▼ *During the blessing of the marriage, the groom covered the bride's head and shoulders with the shawl he wore while praying. This formed a huppah, a canopy that symbolized their new life together under one roof.*

Birth and Death

In medieval times, having children was the most important part of family life, but it was often a difficult process. As many as one in five women died during childbirth, and one-third of children born died before the age of five from illness or injury.

The Birth

Female friends and relatives, and sometimes a skilled assistant called a midwife, helped and encouraged the mother while she was giving birth. The newborn baby was wiped clean, then swaddled, or tightly wrapped in linen cloths. Swaddling kept the baby calm and warm, and some people believed that it kept a newborn's soft limbs in the proper position. The baby's gums were rubbed with honey to ensure that its first taste of life was sweet.

▲ *Children were born at home, with only women present.*

The Baptism

A baptism is a ceremony that welcomes a child into the **Catholic** Church. The baptism usually took place shortly after the child was born. Godparents, who were relatives or close friends, held the baby at the ceremony and promised to help raise the child as a good Christian. Then, the baby's name was announced. Names were often chosen to honor relatives, and were usually those of Christian **saints**.

◀ *During the baptism, the baby was dipped in holy water and blessed by the priest.*

Birthdays

Most medieval people did not celebrate birthdays since exact calendar dates were rarely used. People usually only knew the closest Church holy day. A woman might say, for example, that she was born "three days after the Feast of the Nativity." People in many parts of Europe, especially in the north, celebrated the **feast day** of the saint for whom they were named. They enjoyed a festive meal with their families and godparents, and wealthy or important people received gifts.

At the End of Life

Almost everyone in the Middle Ages died at home with their family present. Whenever possible, a priest performed a final ritual shortly before a person's death. He touched the dying person's eyes, ears, nose, mouth, feet, and hands with special oil, heard his or her last **confession**, and told the person that his or her **sins** were forgiven. The dying person often dictated his **will** at this time, with the priest among the witnesses.

Older women in the community helped prepare a person's body for burial. The deceased was washed and wrapped in a plain fabric called a shroud. Two or three days later, the body was placed in a wooden coffin and carried to the local church in a procession. Many funerals, which were held at the church, were very simple, with the **clergy** saying brief prayers for the dead. Some people made arrangements in their wills for more elaborate rituals, such as full funeral Masses.

▶ *After the funeral service, the body was carried to the graveyard. Sometimes, the body was removed from the coffin so that the coffin could be reused.*

Winter Festivities

During the Middle Ages, the year was full of holidays, most of which were religious. These festivities brightened winter's chilly days and long, dark nights.

The Christmas Season

Celebrations for Christmas began on the evening of December 24, Christmas Eve. The festivities lasted until January 6, a holiday called the Feast of the Epiphany.

There were many ways to mark the beginning of Christmas. In northern Europe, a large tree was cut down and trimmed of branches. The tree, or log, was called the Yule log. It was dragged to the main hearth or fireplace. The bottom end of the Yule log was laid in the hearth and set on fire. As the log burned away over the Christmas season, it was slowly pushed further into the fire until it was gone.

▲ *Christmas, or the Feast of the Nativity, commemorates the birth of Jesus Christ.*

▼ *The Christmas season was the most popular time for masked dances and pageants.*

26

The Feast of the Epiphany

In the Middle Ages, the Feast of the Epiphany was as popular as Christmas. Epiphany celebrates the arrival of three wise men bearing gifts for the baby Jesus. The eve of the Feast of the Epiphany, called Twelfth Night, became the main gift-giving holiday in medieval times.

Small cakes were baked for the festive meal celebrating Epiphany. Hidden inside one cake was a prize, such as a dried pea or bean, or a little jewel or coin. Whoever received the prize became the king or queen of the feast, and pretended to be in charge.

The Feast of Fools

In medieval Europe, the Feast of Fools gave the poor and those with little power a chance to make fun of those above them in rank. In some regions, including most of France, this tradition was celebrated on January 1. On this day, the poorest workers dressed up as lords and **bishops**. Pretending they were of higher rank, the workers gave orders to those normally above them in the social order, and poked fun at those in power. Church leaders, mayors, and city councilors found this tradition disrespectful. They tried to put an end to the Feast of Fools, but it remained popular for centuries.

New Year's Day

Different regions celebrated New Year's Day on different days of the year. Most of medieval Europe considered March 25 the beginning of the New Year. This date marked an important religious holiday called the Feast of the Annunciation. Elsewhere, New Year's Day was celebrated on December 25, January 1, or March 1.

▲ *Medieval people worked less in the winter because of the cold and because there were fewer hours of daylight. People enjoyed their free time playing in the snow, skating on frozen rivers, and visiting friends and family.*

Spring Holidays

Winter's holidays ended with the beginning of Lent. Lent is a 40-day period of prayer and fasting that prepares Christians for Easter.

▲ Carnival is the period immediately before Lent. The word "carnival" means "putting aside meat." Carnival time was the last chance until after Easter to eat foods such as butter, meat, and sweets, and to dance, make music, and play games.

During Lent, people were not supposed to eat meat, sweets, or fatty foods. Simple meals were prepared from beans, lentils, and dried, salted fish. People were expected to attend Mass frequently, and no weddings could take place.

Easter

Easter is the most important holy day of the Christian year. It commemorates Jesus Christ's crucifixion, or death on the cross, and his resurrection, or return to life.

The week preceding Easter, called Holy Week, was full of important rituals. Palm Sunday, the Sunday before Easter, recalls the arrival of Jesus in Jerusalem, a city in present-day Israel. The people welcomed Jesus by spreading palm branches in his path. On Palm Sunday, medieval priests and worshipers marched in processions to local churches, carrying palm and other green branches and singing **hymns**. The priests blessed the branches outside the churches, and families laid them over the tombs of their relatives in churchyards.

Maundy Thursday and Easter Friday

On the Thursday before Easter, called Maundy Thursday in England, a solemn evening Mass remembered Jesus Christ's last meal with his disciples, or followers. On the next day, Easter Friday, processions were held in the streets to mark the day Jesus was crucified.

On Easter Sunday, every Christian was required to attend Mass and take **Communion**. Beautiful decorations and an elaborate service, which included music written especially for Easter Sunday, showed the importance of this holiday.

May Day

The first day of May has an ancient connection with love, **fertility**, and the renewed growth of plants and trees. In the Middle Ages, young people went a-maying, or into woods and meadows to collect wildflowers and tree branches. They sometimes used these cuttings to decorate a tall pole, called a Maypole. The trimmings were tied on with bright ribbons or cords. In some parts of Europe, people danced around the Maypole, weaving together the long strands of ribbon.

▼ *To celebrate May Day, richly dressed nobles rode out on fine horses to gather flowers and to picnic in the woods and fields.*

Harvest Time

Late summer brought the harvest season. Since before Christian times, people in many regions had celebrated August 1 as the traditional beginning of the harvest. In the Middle Ages, August 1 became a holiday called Lammas, or loaf-mass. On this day, the first bread made from the new season's grain was brought to the church and blessed.

Bringing in the harvest required days of labor from dawn to dusk. When the hard work was over for the season, it was the custom to celebrate with a lavish feast. Tables were set up outside. Pigs were roasted and served along with dishes made from local fruits and vegetables. The feast continued long into the night with singing and dancing.

The grain is brought to the barn for threshing, or separating the seeds from the straw.

The tightly fitted sides of the wooden cart kept precious grains from falling out.

Wildflowers and decorated sheaves of wheat trimmed the cart and the oxen's yoke, or collar.

Musicians played
lively music.

Men and women
celebrated after working
hard in the fields,
stacking and binding
sheaves of grain.

Ale made from
grain and hops, the
dried flowers of the
hop vine, was the
main beverage at
the feast.

Glossary

archer A soldier trained to use a bow and arrow

bishop A high-ranking religious leader in the Catholic Church

Catholic Relating to Catholicism, a branch of Christianity

Christianity The religion that follows the teachings of God and Jesus Christ, who Christians believe is God's son

clergy Religious leaders

Communion A Christian ceremony in which a person receives holy bread and wine

confession The act of admitting to one's sins

court A noble's family, household, or supporters

embroider To make a design in cloth using a needle and thread

feast day A day that honors a particular saint

fertility The ability to produce abundant crops or vegetation

habit A long, woolen gown worn by a monk or a nun

heir A person who receives something from another person when that person dies

hymn A song that praises God

Islam A religion based on the teachings of God, whom Muslims call Allah, and his prophets

Judaism A religion whose followers believe in one God and follow the teachings of a holy book called the Torah

lance A long, wooden pole with a sharp iron or steel head

Middle East The region made up of southwestern Asia and northern Africa

modesty Proper behavior and dress

moral Relating to the idea of what is right and wrong

Persian The language of the people of Iran

pikeman A soldier who fights with a long pointed stick called a pike

priest A person who leads religious ceremonies in the Catholic Church

ransom Money paid to free a prisoner

ritual Relating to a religious ceremony, in which steps are performed in a certain order

saint A Christian holy person

savory Salty or spicy, rather than sweet

sermon A speech given as part of a religious service

sin A thought or action that goes against God's wishes

spin To make thread or yarn

spit A skewer or thin rod that holds meat over a fire

tunic A loose garment that extends to the knee and is usually worn with a belt

virtue A valuable quality

will A document containing a person's wishes with regard to his or her property after his or her death

Index

birth 24

birthdays 25

books of manners 4, 5, 9, 10, 18

children 8–9, 18, 24

chivalry 4, 12-15

cleanliness 11

clothing 4, 5, 18, 19, 21

feasts 8, 10–11, 23, 25, 26, 27, 30–31

funerals 25

holidays 4, 5, 26–29

knights 4, 6, 8, 12–15

manners 4, 5, 8, 9, 10–11, 12, 17, 18, 19

monasteries 4, 16–17

nobles 4, 5, 6, 8–9, 12, 13, 14, 15, 18, 20, 21, 23, 29

oaths 4, 6, 7, 13

peasants 4, 5, 6, 7, 20, 23

religions 4, 5, 6, 11, 12, 13, 16–17, 18, 22, 23, 24, 25, 26, 27, 28, 29, 30

samurai 14

tournaments 15

weddings 4, 18, 20–23, 28

wills 25

women 9, 15, 16, 17, 18–19, 20, 21, 22, 23, 24, 25

1 2 3 4 5 6 7 8 9 0 Printed in the U.S.A. 2 1 0 9 8 7 6 5